Practice in the Basic Skills

Contents

Picture vocabulary

Write the names of these **mammals**.

Write a short description of any **five** of them.

Pronouns

A Write out the **pronouns** in the following sentences.

1 Connor thinks he is the best swimmer in the school.

2 We caught the boys and they admitted stealing the apples.

3 He saw me and he returned the book.

4 I thanked her and she gave it to me.

5 Please pass them to me.

6 She asked whether they would be able to go with her.

7 When you have read this book please pass it on to him.

8 They told him that they would meet us at 10 o'clock.

9 She said that it belonged to her.

10 He was given 50p but he lost it.

B Use a **pronoun** to show **possession** instead of the words in the brackets.

1 This ball is (belongs to my sister).

2 This bicycle is (belongs to me).

3 This rabbit is (belongs to my sister and me).

4 This cricket bat is (belongs to my brother).

5 This wheelbarrow is (belongs to my neighbours).

6 This tennis racket is (belongs to you).

C Complete these sentences by adding the correct **pronoun**.

1 The girls hurried so that _____ would not miss the train.

2 Aled's mother asked _____ to cut the grass.

3 The dog buried a bone and could not find _____ .

4 As my friend and I walked towards the river, a policeman stopped _____ .

5 Will _____ please tell Mrs Clark that Sophie will collect _____ shopping?

Alphabetical order

A Write the names of these objects in **alphabetical order**. Look at the **second** letter.

1

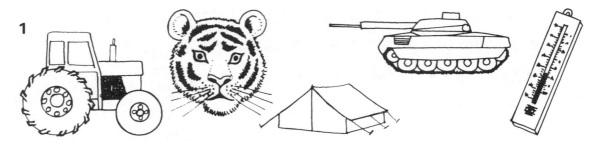

Do the same with these words.

2	pull	pity	pygmy	pan	polish	plum
3	hymn	help	hobby	hawk	high	huge
4	fear	foot	funny	field	fair	flat
5	witch	wrote	whirl	worm	wash	week

B Write the names of these objects in **alphabetical order**. Look at the **third** letter.

1

Do the same with these words.

2	bay	bath	banana	basket	baboon	barley
3	fan	fail	fast	family	factory	fall
4	ham	hatch	hair	hawk	harp	habit
5	meat	merge	message	mend	mellow	meet

C Write these words in **alphabetical order**, looking at the **fourth** letter.

1	forward	forfeit	fork	forbid	form	forget
2	paternal	path	patter	patch	patrol	patience
3	canvas	cane	canyon	candid	cancel	canoe
4	manly	mankind	mansion	manager	mane	manor

Picture vocabulary

Write the names of these **means of transport**.

Write a short description of any **five** of them.

Vocabulary – associations

A   What do you associate with each of the following?

1	an aquarium	**5**	a hangar	**9**	a reservoir
2	barracks	**6**	an aviary	**10**	a refinery
3	a museum	**7**	an orchard	**11**	a hold
4	a silo	**8**	a studio	**12**	a vineyard

B   Place these people in the positions of authority each holds.

ᏋᎢ done

> **keeper**   **editor**   **director**   **president**
> **conductor**   **headteacher**   **captain**   **judge**
> **governor**   **principal**

1 .... of a school   **6** .... of a prison

2 .... of a ship   **7** .... of a republic

3 .... of a college   **8** .... of a newspaper

4 .... of animals in a zoo   **9** .... of a court of law

5 .... of a firm or company   **10** .... of an orchestra

C   What special names are given to books which contain:

Marus done

1   the meanings of words?

2   the story of a persons life?

3   a collection of maps?

4   a record of daily happenings?

5   a collection of poems?

6   a detailed, daily record of a ship's progress?

7   pictures, newspaper cuttings, etc.?

8   facts about many kinds of knowledge?

9   telephone numbers?

10   a collection of postage stamps?

Verbs – sounds

A Choose **verbs** which convey a **sound** to complete these sentences.

1 Steam .... from the damaged radiator.

2 The car wheels .... on the loose stones.

3 At dawn, in the forest, the birds .... happily.

4 During the storm hailstones .... against the windows.

5 The glass .... when the cricket ball hit the window.

6 The rusty hinges on the castle door .... loudly.

B Complete the following by using **sound** words.

1 The .... of water.

2 The .... of an explosion.

3 The .... of leaves.

4 The .... of a rifle.

5 The .... of a bell.

6 The .... of paper.

7 The .... of hoofs.

8 The .... of donkeys.

C Complete these.

1 The boom of a ....

2 The howling of ....

3 The slam of a ....

4 The clanking of ....

5 The hoot of an ....

6 The shuffle of ....

7 The wail of a ....

8 The throb of an ....

D Complete these by adding a sentence which shows the **cause** of the sound.

1 Splash!

2 Whoosh!

3 Rat-tat-tat!

4 Bang! Crash!

Spelling

These words have either **ei** or **ie** missing. Write them out correctly.

1	w __ __ ght	**5**	misch __ __ f	**9**	for __ __ gn	**13**	s __ __ ze
2	n __ __ ce	**6**	dec __ __ ve	**10**	r __ __ ndeer	**14**	cash __ __ r
3	n __ __ ghbour	**7**	retr __ __ ve	**11**	anc __ __ nt	**15**	conc __ __ t
4	shr __ __ k	**8**	c __ __ ling	**12**	rec __ __ pt	**16**	ch __ __ f

Vocabulary

Rewrite these sentences replacing the words in bold type with words of your own.

1   After the long walk Jayne slept **like a log**.

2   I shouldn't like to be **in your shoes**!

3   It's **touch and go** whether the dam bursts.

4   Old Mrs Baxter is finding it difficult to **make both ends meet**.

5   It rained **cats and dogs** most of our holiday.

6   I'm always **hard up** before the end of the week.

Punctuation

Write out the following sentences putting in all the necessary **commas, full stops** and **capital letters**.

1   clive paul and craig play golf every saturday and sunday

2   mrs marsden told jasmine to take the cakes to aunty margaret

3   in our easter holidays we went to london and saw buckingham palace and the bank of england

4   his friends who were becoming anxious telephoned leeds police station a police officer soon arrived

5   for sunday lunch billy and rob had pork chops cabbage carrots and roast potatoes

Abbreviations

What do the following **abbreviations** stand for?

1   NSPCC   4   Co.   7   IMF   10   GM
2   USA   5   RNIB   8   NATO   11   Ltd
3   RNLI   6   WWF   9   UK   12   Km

Opposites

Write the **opposites** of these words.

1   depart   5   rapid   9   majority ....
2   seldom   6   minimum   10   moving ....
3   wealth   7   barren   11   legal ....
4   guilty   8   retreat   12   internal ....

Synonyms

Write words which are **similar in meaning** to these.

1   commence   5   gigantic   9   permit ....
2   expensive   6   horizontal   10   abandon ....
3   exterior   7   ferocious   11   duplicate ....
4   remedy   8   insolent   12   transparent ....

Homonyms

For each of the following words write another word which **sounds exactly the same** but is spelt differently.

1   sore   5   root   9   isle ....
2   medal   6   wait   10   principle ....
3   key   7   bridle   11   doe ....
4   rap   8   pedal   12   ceiling ....

9

Adjectives

A Choose a suitable **adjective** to complete the following phrases.

e.g. a <u>steep</u> hill

1   a _____ book   6   a _____ winter

2   a _____ car   7   some _____ trees

3   the _____ cliffs   8   a _____ holiday

4   a _____ party   9   the _____ mountaineer

5   the _____ river   10 a _____ storm

B These lines of words are all adjectives. Write out the adjective which has the **strongest** meaning.

e.g. fierce, wild, <u>brutal</u>, cruel, unfair

1   large, huge, big, gigantic, sizeable

2   shiny, clear, brilliant, bright, glowing

3   attractive, lovely, nice, pretty, beautiful

4   sad, unhappy, discouraged, miserable, down

5   cool, chilly, nippy, icy, wintry

6   tall, high, lofty, towering, elevated

C Rewrite the following phrases, choosing an **opposite** to the adjective in each phrase.

1   a patient driver   7   an ordinary holiday

2   a harmful sting   8   a temporary building

3   a rude boy   9   the maximum score

4   the interior walls   10 the optimistic girl

5   a blunt knife   11 a counterfeit bank note

6   the alert guard dog   12 the opaque glass

Spelling and vocabulary

A   All these answers begin with **s** and have something to do with the sea.

1   a plant which grows in the sea   s __ __ __ __ __ __

2   a lot of fish swimming together   s __ __ __ __

3   an underwater ship   s __ __ __ __ __ __ __ __

4   a large fish with rows of sharp teeth   s __ __ __ __

5   a swimmer using flippers and a mask   s __ __ __ __

__ __ __ __ __

B   All these answers begin with **ex**.

1   Plenty of _____ is good for your health.

2   Dr Livingstone _____ parts of the African continent.

3   The runways were _____ so that bigger jets could land.

4   The dentist _____ two of my teeth.

5   You can't expect me to buy that bicycle, it's too _____ .

C   Write the **group name** for each of the following collections.

1   lemon, peach, plum, lime, apple, orange

2   onion, lettuce, cabbage, leek, turnip, bean

3   square, hexagon, triangle, rectangle, octagon

4   lead, zinc, aluminium, gold, platinum

5   Arctic, Pacific, Atlantic, Indian, Antarctic

D   Add two words which belong to each of these **groups** of words.

1   crocus, narcissus, hyacinth, snowdrop

2   golf, squash, tennis, rounders

3   Venus, Earth, Mars, Pluto

4   Sophia, Saira, Stella, Sabrina

5   eagle, vulture, owl, hawk

Vocabulary

A   All these are worn on the head.

What are they? Who would wear them?

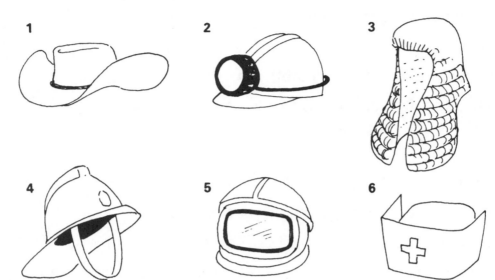

B   Write the word which names each of these groups.

    1   rye, barley, oats, wheat, maize

    2   BBC, YHA, JP, BSc, PTO

    3   pike, roach, perch, carp, tench

    4   Smith, Aitken, Hughes, Ahmed, O'Hara

    5   hamster, beaver, rabbit, mouse, squirrel

    6   grasshopper, fly, butterfly, wasp, ladybird

    7   parsley, bay, thyme, sage, rosemary

    8   mahogany, teak, oak, walnut, beech

C   What is the name of:

    1   a room where typists and clerks work?

    2   the room where meals are cooked on board a ship?

    3   the room in a bank where money and valuables are kept?

    4   a small room used for sleeping on board a ship?

    5   a room where prisoners are kept in prison?

Indirect speech

Change these sentences to **indirect speech**.

1   "My football boots need new laces," said Danny.

2   The policewoman said to my dad, "You aren't allowed to park your car in this street."

3   "Has the train to Walsall gone?" asked Heather.

4   Aunty Shirley said to me, "I hope you like your birthday present."

5   I said to the librarian, "Have you a copy of *Oliver Twist*?"

6   Marian said, "I go swimming twice a week."

7   "I am afraid, Bobby," snapped Mr Toms, "that you are not working hard enough to pass the exam."

8   "Freya," asked the teacher, "will you bring the tape recorder, please?"

9   "Come on, slow coach," shouted George. "We'll miss the bus if we don't hurry."

10   "I'm sorry, George, but I'm running as fast as I can," said Milly.

Present and past tense

Copy and complete this table.

	present tense	past tense		present tense	past tense
1	give		11		threw
2	know		12		forgot
3	catch		13		built
4	feel		14		rang
5	leave		15		stole
6	swim		16		brought
7	strike		17		held
8	lie		18		shook
9	begin		19		drove
10	drink		20		flew

Direct speech

Change these sentences to **direct speech**.

1   Simon asked me how tall I was.

2   My mum wanted to know if I was ready for tea.

3   Elizabeth shouted to Saira to be quick.

4   The mechanic told Mr Barnes that his car would be ready on Tuesday.

5   Tilly's mother asked her if she had finished her homework.

6   Paul told his dad that he had been chosen to play for the school cricket team.

7   Dean asked Mark whether he wanted to go fishing with him.

8   Mrs Bladen told her son, Andrew, that he must not miss the last bus home.

9   Harry Cox shouted that he was trapped on his roof.

10   Mr Green asked David to clean the windows and brush the floor.

Incorrect sentences

Rewrite these sentences correctly.

1   The dog and the cat was lying on the carpet.

2   Malcolm learned me to play badminton.

3   Was it her or him which spoke to you ?

4   Dawn could not see her dog nowhere.

5   You can lend my bicycle if you're careful.

6   Patrick catched too perch in the canal.

7   The reward was divided between the three boy's.

8   Have you spoke to your father?

9   My brother were taller.

10   Neither the boys nor the girls has finished there work.

Picture story

Look carefully at the six pictures.

Write a story, in six paragraphs, that is interesting, exciting and has a humorous ending.

Contractions

Write out these **contractions** in full.

1	mustn't	**6**	who'd	**11**	won't
2	that's	**7**	where's	**12**	they'll
3	I'll	**8**	wouldn't	**13**	there'd
4	we've	**9**	she'll	**14**	it's
5	you're	**10**	they've	**15**	we'll

Vocabulary

Choose the correct word from the brackets to complete these sentences.

1 Melissa _____ her homework as soon as she came home.   (done, did)

2 Billy and Danny _____ an exciting film last night.   (saw, seen)

3 Do you know _____ is coming to see us?   (who, whom)

4 You and _____ will have to cut the old lady's lawn.   (me, I)

5 Did you borrow _____ books from the library?   (them, those)

6 Will you _____ me to play squash?   (teach, learn)

7 The farmer wondered _____ his cattle _____ .   (were, where)

8 Have you _____ Freya? Yes, I _____ her getting on a bus. (saw, seen)

9 The football captain wants to see you and _____ .   (me, I)

10 It's _____ late _____ go out with your _____ friends. (to, two, too)

Adjectives

Use the correct form of the **adjective** in the brackets to complete these sentences.

1 Spain is a _____ country than Britain.   (warm)

2 Jonathan did _____ work than Wayne.   (little)

3 Sarah is the _____ _____ member of our class.   (honest)

4 Bobby is the _____ of the two brothers.   (clever)

5 Of all the rooms in our house this is the _____ .   (cosy)

6 Mrs Arnold is _____ _____ than her sister.   (generous)

Plurals

Rewrite these sentences in the **plural** form.

1   Yesterday the workman repaired the roof.

2   I saw a calf, a horse, a goose and a donkey on the farm.

3   The policewoman caught the thief in the act.

4   The old lady twisted her ankle on the stony beach.

5   The boy fell off the rock and hurt himself.

6   My cousin came to see me last weekend.

7   The girl's pencil was in the box.

8   The school play wasn't very well acted.

9   The postman delivered a letter and a parcel to the house in the valley.

10   I do not think you understand the problem.

Spelling

There is **one spelling mistake** in each of these sentences. Find it and write the word correctly.

1   We all laughed at the puppy's behavior.

2   Jenny was very tearfull when she fell off her bicycle.

3   I saw the rabbit dissappear down that hole.

4   Neither John nor Betty has compleated the work.

5   The policeman siezed the frightened dog.

6   Allthough he was near exhaustion, Oliver finished the race.

7   Heather replied sensably to the teacher's questions.

8   There was a beatiful display of roses in the entrance hall.

9   In warm weather Amelia allways wears sandals.

10   Mum knitted a woolen jumper.

Vocabulary – verb association

A   Pair each **verb** in column A with its correct meaning from column B.

   A

   1   to conceal

   2   to demolish

   3   to substitute

   4   to suppress

   5   to excavate

   6   to investigate

   7   to erupt

   8   to refine

...ith another

B   Complete these sentences by choosing the most suitable verb formed from those in column A above.

   1   The troops .... the rebellion by firing on the mob.

   2   Lava and ashes .... from the volcano.

   3   The archaeologists .... part of an ancient buried city.

   4   Sugar, oil and metals are .... before being used.

   5   Our goalkeeper, Colin, was injured and Alex was ....

C   Of which **animal** does the person speaking remind you, in each of these sentences?

   1   "My throat is very sore. I can hardly swallow," **croaked** Graham.

   2   Mr Ash **bellowed**, "Keep off my grass or I'll get the police."

   3   The fans **screamed** with delight when their favourite boy band appeared.

   4   My uncle Jim **droned** on and on about his family's history.

   5   The huge crowd **roared** when the leader of the marathon entered the stadium.

18

Spelling and vocabulary

A   Who are the following people? All the answers end in **ist**.

1   someone who plays a piano

2   someone who knows about science

3   a person who writes novels

4   someone who drops from an aircraft by parachute

5   a person who makes a doll appear to speak

6   someone who sings songs alone

7   a person who looks on the bright side of things

B   The answers to these clues all begin with **att**.

1   a room in the roof of a house

2   to try to do something

3   to start a fight

4   pleasing to look at

5   to fasten; to join

C   The answers to these clues all end with **ture**.

1   a hole made with something pointed

2   the measure of how hot or cold something is

3   to take a prisoner

4   articles needed in a home, e.g. chairs, beds

5   to cause very much pain

D   The answers to these clues have **rr** in them.

1   to disagree; to argue angrily

2   a looking glass

3   to give in

4   a small dog

5   a place where stone is obtained from the ground

Analogies

Complete these **analogies**.

1 Kennel is to dog as _____ is to horse.

2 _____ is to rabbit as wool is to sheep.

3 Elephant is to _____ as pig is to grunts.

4 Gander is to goose as ram is to _____ .

5 Hind is to fawn as _____ is to leveret.

6 Beaver is to lodge as badger is to _____ .

7 Snake is to _____ as frog is to croak.

8 _____ is to scales as bird is to feathers.

Verbs

Rewrite the following sentences by choosing a **verb** which means the same as the words in bold type.

1 Don't tease that guard dog or it may **go for** you.

2 Karen is **going through** a lot of pain because of her broken tooth.

3 Stephen **goes in for** every chess tournament in the district.

4 Dogs often **go after** cats.

5 The council are determined to **go through with** their plan to build a new bridge.

6 Shops have sales when prices of goods **go down**.

Vocabulary

Use **one word** to express each of the following.

1 cheering and clapping

2 the highest point

3 someone who watches a game

4 a very great shortage of food

5 a slow-moving river of ice

Pronouns

A Complete these sentences by choosing one of the **pronouns** from this list.

yourselves	himself	myself	yourself	herself

1 "Are you sure you wrote this story .... , Jen?"

2 "I can manage to lift it .... , thank you."

3 "All right, you and Freddie may stay, but you must make .... useful."

4 Jayne enjoyed .... at the party.

5 Tom fell awkwardly and hurt ....

B Each of these sentences contains one **pronoun**. Write it down and the **noun(s)** it replaces.

1 "You may come out now," Mrs Morris said to Steven.

2 The storm had stopped but it caused a lot of damage.

3 Paul and Sally worked on until they had finished painting the kitchen.

4 Jacqueline asked Mia to lend her £5.00.

5 "Listen to me, children," said Mr Morris.

C Write the correct **pronoun** in singular or plural form.

	singular	plural		singular	plural
1	I		6		ours
2	myself		7		us
3	it		8		their
4	hers		9		yourselves
5	me		10		themselves

Contractions

Write these sentences using a **contraction** in place of the words in bold type.

1 **Where have** you been since tea?

2 Ewan **does not** play rugby anymore.

3 **You would** be better if you practised more.

4 My dog **will not** obey me.

5 You **cannot** get in the concert without a ticket.

6 I **do not** know where Patrick has gone.

7 **I would** be very pleased if **you would** work harder.

8 I **shall not** be able to go fishing tomorrow.

9 **I will** see if **they are** ready to start.

10 **They have** had their chance so **it is** up to you to take yours.

Incorrect sentences

Write these sentences correctly.

1 My brother learned me how to ride a bike.

2 Ava acted good in the play.

3 Seamus wouldn't give me none of his toffees.

4 There is a lot of mountains in Austria.

5 Terry ran home as quick as he could.

6 A man and his dog was waiting outside the shop.

7 Betsy could not come no quicker.

8 Your fishing rod is different to mine.

9 He want to go tomorrow.

10 The group sung the same song twice.

11 Poor Lesley couldn't remember nothing.

12 Between you and I, I don't think he is the right choice for captain.

Vocabulary

Underline the one word in each line which stands for all the other words.

1 sympathy   love   pity   anger   rage   feeling   hate

2 jumping   skating   running   exercising   swimming   walking

3 sapphire   ruby   gem   opal   diamond   emerald

4 flat   house   dwelling   bungalow   maisonette   apartment

5 tomorrow   time   afternoon   evening   today   yesterday

Jumbled letters

Here are six pictures of birds. Name them by rearranging the groups of letters – they are not below the correct pictures.

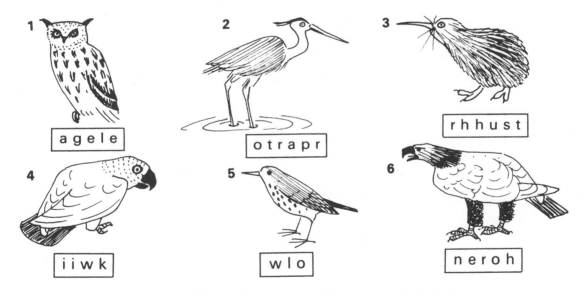

1 a g e l e

2 o t r a p r

3 r h h u s t

4 i i w k

5 w l o

6 n e r o h

Associations

Write the following words in pairs that go together.

set A			**set B**	
1	photographer	whistle	1	actress	laboratory
2	jockey	baton	2	keeper	kitchen
3	referee	spanner	3	chemist	office
4	doctor	camera	4	astronomer	studio
5	conductor	brush	5	administrator	theatre
6	mechanic	saddle	6	chef	observatory
7	decorator	stethoscope	7	artist	zoo

Adverbs

A   Write out the **adverbs** in these sentences.

1   Peter plays golf regularly.

2   Sophie looked dejectedly at her damaged bicycle and started to cry loudly.

3   I am coming now but I must go soon.

4   "The circus is held twice daily," shouted Tom excitedly.

5   "Put it there!" Ian ordered angrily.

6   "Have you looked everywhere?" asked Liam sadly.

7   "I cannot find your puppy anywhere," answered Megan sadly.

8   Tom has always been a good batsman and he bowls well too.

9   All the deer ran away into the woods when they heard us shouting loudly.

10   I once saw a fisherman catch a huge salmon which struggled frantically to escape.

11   "We have never met before," replied Harriet.

12   They have to run twice round the park.

B   Choose suitable **adverbs** to complete the following.

1   The teacher explained ....

2   Our team lost ....

3   Mark answered ....

4   I remember ....

5   We visit Cardiff ....

6   The injured men staggered ....

7   The baby chuckled ....

8   She spoke ....

9   The rude boy sneered ....

10   The cyclist was injured ....

11   Laura listened ....

12   They arrived ....

13   Our team won ....

14   The lost dog wandered ....

15   The hungry boy ate his food ....

16   The two ladies waited ....

Opposites

Rewrite these sentences, changing **one word** in each sentence to give the **opposite** meaning.

Do not use <u>was not</u> or <u>wasn't</u>, etc.

1   Alan's invention was a failure.
2   The yacht sailed through the rough seas.
3   Sarah checked the time as she left the office.
4   It was possible for the mountain to be climbed.
5   Bobby admitted that he had left the tap running.
6   The passengers were very patient when the plane was delayed.
7   Our teacher was discouraged by our exam results.
8   About one third of Jayne's answers were correct.
9   The majority of our class come to school by bus.
10 Tom helped his dad to push the car forwards.

Vocabulary

Rewrite the following sentences by choosing **one word** instead of those in bold type.

1   We managed to **put out** the fire.
2   Workmen have **put up** a bus shelter in our street.
3   You can do it! Don't be **put off** by their failure.
4   You will have to **put aside** some money for your holidays.
5   The old lady couldn't **put up with** the loud noise of the machines any longer.
6   After losing a sail in a violent storm, the yacht **put into** port for repairs.
7   Sally was **put out** by the way her friends behaved towards her.
8   The football match was **put off** because of the frozen ground.

Verbs

These fifteen verbs end in **ate**.

celebrate	**rotate**	**hesitate**	**meditate**	**elevate**
lubricate	**emigrate**	**narrate**	**associate**	**relate**
cultivate	**educate**	**germinate**	**imitate**	**dilate**

The meanings of **ten** of these verbs now follow. Match these meanings correctly with the verbs.

1   to oil or grease machinery

2   to tell the story of

3   to think quietly

4   to prepare and use soil for crops

5   to make or become larger or wider

6   to do the same as someone else

7   to turn like a wheel

8   to help people to learn; to teach

9   to tell; give an account of

10   to leave own country and settle in another

Completing sentences

In each of the following sentences there are two dashes. Choose suitable words from this list to complete the sentences.

so, that	**such, that**	**neither, nor**	**whether, or**	**if, then**	**either, or**

1   _____ my sister _____ my brother has had chicken pox.

2   I am fishing this afternoon, _____ you come with me _____ not.

3   _____ you stay in wet clothes _____ of course you'll be ill.

4   It was _____ a poor film _____ I came out after half an hour.

5   _____ Darren will finish his work today _____ he will not play football.

6   The book was _____ good _____ I finished it before I went to sleep.

Spelling

Here is a list of twenty words of which **ten** are spelt incorrectly. Find them and write them out correctly.

deceive	memory	modern	foreign	beginning
electricity	Febuary	anxious	seperate	Wedensday
sieze	language	eigth	nuisance	presant
definate	neccessary	skillful	beleive	wriggled

Singular

Rewrite these sentences in the **singular**.

1   The windows have been cleaned.
2   These boys wish to play chess.
3   We were hoping to finish the paintings last Monday.
4   The ladies checked their watches.
5   The policewomen arrested the thieves.
6   We don't think you can catch the mice.
7   Chimpanzees are intelligent animals.
8   Our cousins are coming on holiday with our family.

Completing sentences

Complete the following by adding interesting phrases which tell us **where** something took place.

1   We planted several trees ....
2   There was a raging fire ....
3   There were many fish ....
4   The exhausted climbers spent the night ....
5   The damaged aircraft was forced to land ....
6   A new bus shelter was built ....
7   The football international match took place ....
8   I saw a helicopter rescue the fishermen ....

Spelling

All these answers have **our** in them.

1   not sweet to taste   __ o u r
2   tennis is played on a   __ o u r __
3   a sheltered place where ships are safe   __ __ __ __ o u r
4   someone who writes for newspapers or magazines
    __ o u r __ __ __ __ __ __
5   to help someone to keep on trying   __ __ __ o u r __ __ __
6   a person who lives near you   __ __ __ __ __ __ o u r
7   going from one place to another   __ o u r __ __ __
8   covering to protect the body from injury   __ __ __ o u r

Joining phrases

Join the following pairs of phrases by choosing the most suitable word from those in the brackets.

1   She was very ill (but, and, so) we phoned for the doctor.
2   It is very late (so, but, and) we can still catch the last bus.
3   We must leave now (and, so, or) we shall miss the train.
4   She may be very poor (so, but, or) she is genuine.
5   I have my coat (so, but, because) it doesn't matter if it rains.
6   You make a model your way (although, and, so) I'll make one my way.
7   Sally is a fast runner (because, so, but) she didn't win the race.
8   Darren is very unhappy (but, because, although) he has lost his dog.
9   You don't need to come with us (so, unless, but) you wish to.
10 Holly toasted the bread (but, because, while) Emma boiled the eggs.

Incorrect sentences

Rewrite these sentences correctly.

1   She ran home as quick as she could.
2   My radio battery is wore out.
3   There is a cat and a dog on our front garden.
4   The boy has broke his leg.
5   My fingers ache and I cannot write no more.
6   "Please pass me them books," said Graham.
7   "I seen the boy run over the field," said the caretaker.
8   The teacher thought Michael done it.
9   Wasn't they pleased when they knew we was coming.
10 Every one of us have an equal chance off reaching the final.

Rhyming words

Among these twenty words there are **five** *sets* of **rhyming words** – **four** words in each set. Write out the five sets.

made	home	become	cheer	played
toes	some	near	dome	froze
weighed	foam	crumb	grows	raid
smear	comb	glum	chose	sphere

Questions

Write **two** sets of questions – one **serious** and the other **humorous** – to which the following would be reasonable answers.

1   Three and a half kilometres.
2   Either a bull or a cow.
3   Maths, science and geography.
4   Follow the road to the traffic lights and turn right.
5   Black and white stripes.
6   At midnight.
7   As soon as I have eaten my breakfast.
8   Probably a hockey player or a golfer.
9   It landed in the main street.
10 Jamaica or New Zealand.

Homonyms

Complete the following by choosing the correct word from the brackets.

1   Chloe has _____ her hair blonde.   (died, dyed)
2   Female sheep are _____ .   (ewes, yews)
3   Sam _____ us about his fishing holiday.   (told, tolled)
4   William was _____ for speeding on his motorbike.   (find, fined)
5   Dad has _____ many kinds of vegetable seeds this year.   (sown, sewn)
6   The _____ is a part of your foot.   (heel, heal)
7   Mum has _____ two badges on my coat.   (sown, sewn)
8   We are going to football _____ tonight.   (practise, practice)
9   I must _____ shooting with my right foot.   (practise, practice)

Similes

Complete these **similes** – the answers are all **animals**.

1   as stubborn as _____
2   as playful as _____
3   as strong as _____
4   as gentle as _____
5   as proud as _____
6   as blind as _____
7   as swift as _____
8   as wise as _____

Pronouns

Rewrite the following sentences by forming the correct words from those given in brackets.

1 What have you done with (you) fishing rod?

2 On (he) return home Peter could not open the door.

3 Tom's bicycle is clean but (I) is very dirty.

4 Our friends have a new car. Ours is smaller than (they).

5 I have lost my dictionary. Will you lend me (you)?

6 The bus was damaged but (it) passengers were unhurt.

7 Alex and Oliver left on their journey after saying goodbye to (they) friends.

8 Jenny wanted to borrow (I) bicycle to go to the shops.

9 Those aren't your football boots. They are (me).

10 (We) netball team won all (it) matches in the league.

your or you're

Complete these sentences by writing either **your** or **you're**.

1 Please tell me when .... ready to begin.

2 You should help .... mother more often.

3 Do .... feet ache when .... running the cross country?

4 If .... coming, bring .... bat and wickets.

5 I think .... improving but .... still not ready to take .... place in the team.

Vocabulary

Write out the word which is **out of place** in these groups of words.

1 hamster gerbil cat rat mouse

2 regulate adjust modify vary replace

3 conclude cease halt commence terminate

4 brother nephew cousin son father

5 speed rush hurry stroll hasten

6 climb descend decline drop fall

7 trip voyage hotel journey excursion

8 daffodil grass crocus tulip snowdrop

9 hail rain sleet snow heat

10 pine cedar holly ash yew

Verbs

A   Make a list of **verbs** in these sentences.

   1   She offered to lend me her tennis racket.

   2   Andrew ran well and finished second.

   3   Devina called at her aunty's before she went to school.

   4   My dog comes to me when I whistle.

   5   "Run away and play in the park," suggested Dad.

   6   In the morning Syed ate his breakfast, then dug the garden, cut the grass and trimmed the hedge.

   7   "Come and read to me," said the teacher.

   8   The trawler was tossed about in the storm and struck the rocks and sank.

   9   Fiona rode her bicycle to school but she fell off and cut her arm.

  10   The tall striker swerved past the centre half and scored a brilliant goal.

B   Write the **verbs** which match the following meanings. The first letter of each verb is given.

   1   to cry w.............................

   2   to make better again c.............................

   3   to go on foot w.............................

   4   to feel t.............................

   5   to go up in the air r.............................

   6   to make a noise like a duck q.............................

   7   to hit with the foot k.............................

   8   to walk through water w.............................

   9   to turn round and round t.............................

  10   to hear carefully l.............................

  11   to turn like a wheel r.............................

  12   to do as you are told o.............................

  13   to repair m.............................

  14   to hold tightly g.............................

  15   to end; to complete f.............................

  16   to walk slowly a.............................

  17   to take away s.............................

  18   to buy p.............................

  19   to eat in small bites n.............................

  20   to give up s.............................

Adjectives

A   Write out the **adjectives** in these sentences.

    1   The downcast team walked off the muddy field after losing their first match.

    2   The two considerate children helped the elderly lady across the busy street.

    3   Continuous rain made the sandy beach a dismal sight.

    4   The four experienced climbers succeeded in climbing the sheer, slippery rock-face.

    5   An impressive welcome awaited the three triumphant American balloonists after their successful crossing of the vast Atlantic.

    6   Heavy grey clouds darkened the sky and torrential rain followed quickly to ruin the exciting game of cricket.

B   Write down the strongest **adjective** in each group.

    1   sore, uncomfortable, tender, agonizing, painful

    2   disobedient, naughty, wicked, mischievous, incorrect

    3   fine, good, great, incomparable, fair, valuable

    4   sizeable, big, large, great, giant, colossal

    5   interesting, gorgeous, pretty, handsome, charming

C   Make the meanings of the following nouns more interesting by adding **two adjectives** to each.

e.g. dog ⟶ a black, shaggy dog

1	holiday	**6**	street	**11**	room
2	tree	**7**	smell	**12**	fire
3	mountain	**8**	film	**13**	wind
4	dream	**9**	cat	**14**	neighbour
5	friend	**10**	hobby	**15**	sunset

Spelling

Here is a list of twenty-five words. **Twelve** are spelt incorrectly. Find them and spell them correctly.

library	secondry	generous	leisure	minature
excitement	parallel	calender	marvelous	disagree
dissappear	exaggerate	temprature	interfere	parliment
poisonous	adress	detatch	cautious	courageous
choclate	breakable	terrific	cuboard	miscellanous

Comparing adjectives

e.g. big, bigger, biggest   beautiful, more beautiful, most beautiful.
Complete the table.

	positive	comparative	superlative
1	tall		
2	safe		
3	heavy		
4	noisy		
5	honest		
6	intelligent		
7	good		
8	old		
9	bad		
10	thoughtful		

Vocabulary

A Write **one word only** for each of the following.

1 go into ....
2 go up ....
3 go back ....
4 go down ....
5 go on hands and knees ....
6 go forward ....
7 go away ....
8 go after ....

B Complete the following to make interesting sentences.

1 Arriving at the airport, we ....
2 Browsing round the market, the old lady ....
3 Looking through the door, Roger saw ....
4 Seizing him by the trousers, ...
5 Running down the street, Lauren ....

Comprehension

David's feet were no longer part of him. When he himself cared no more, his feet followed their own path independently, stealing along noiselessly, confidently, guiding his body so that he kept to the shadows and avoided obstacles, stopping him in time, or urging him on whenever he felt he would rather lie down and wait till he was caught. And his feet had carried him over the bridge.

He clenched his teeth. "Salonica!" he whispered and went on repeating the word over and over again to himself until it seemed to fill his brain. "Go south till you reach Salonica. Think of nothing else!"

At that moment the sound of a car pulling up caused him to stiffen. Was he far enough from the road? Then he heard voices. He was so terrified he nearly jumped out of his skin. He was quite unused to the sound of voices by this time; the last he had heard were the guard's and the man's.

But these were different, and they were coming nearer. David relaxed completely so that he would make as little noise as possible, and as he did so he thought that in a moment all would be over – everything.

The men sat down a little way off and lit cigarettes, and it gradually dawned upon David that they were not looking for him at all. He began to listen to what they were saying. He found it difficult to follow them since their speech differed from the man's, but after a while David was able to distinguish words that were familiar to him. They drove a delivery van, like the men who brought supplies to the camp. They were arguing now, but with no great heat: one of them wanted to drive on, and the other wanted to visit someone first in the town David had seen nearby. In the end he got his way; the first man said he would go with him, but only for half an hour as it was a long way home.

Like an echo of his own thoughts, David caught the word 'Salonica'!

From *I am David* by Anne Holm

1a What place was David trying to reach?

b In which direction did this place lie?

2 Would you say David had been travelling for a long time or not? Give a reason for your answer.

3 David appears to be an escaped prisoner. Find two facts from the passage which suggest this.

4 Why was David terrified when he heard voices?

5 What made him realise that the men weren't looking for him?

6 Why did David find it difficult to understand what the men were saying?

7 Where did David think he had seen the van before?

8 What sound caused David to 'stiffen'?

9 Quote three phrases from the passage which suggest that David's feet were moving of their own accord.

10 When and where do you think David's adventure took place?

11 Give a title to this extract.

12 In your own words explain the following phrases.

stealing along
it gradually dawned upon David
with no great heat
like an echo of his own thoughts

13 Write sentences to show that you know the meaning of these words.

avoid   relax   distinguish
clench   differ

14 Pick out the following from the passage.

a	three adverbs	**d**	three pronouns
b	three prepositions	**e**	three verbs
c	three common nouns	**f**	three adjectives

Verbs

Complete each sentence by choosing the most suitable **verb**. Do not use <u>said</u>.

1 "Simon Aitken is the winner of the cross country cup," _____ the principal.

2 "Don't make a sound or they'll find us," _____ Rosie.

3 "Stop! The bridge has collapsed," _____ the policewoman.

4 "I'll win all the races, you'll see," _____ the boy.

5 "It would be much safer if you followed the path," _____ the farmer.

6 "Yes, it was me. I broke the window," _____ Tim.

7 "This class is too noisy. Also you are lazy," _____ the teacher.

8 "I shall have to think carefully about that," _____ Fatima.

Rhyming words

In each of these lines of words pick out the word that **does not** rhyme with the word in bold type.

1	**weight**	hate	wait	height	freight	fête
2	**drain**	main	feign	mane	same	lane
3	**dough**	sew	doe	bough	flow	so
4	**steak**	stake	ache	flake	streak	snake
5	**pair**	pier	pear	care	fair	snare
6	**berth**	earth	worth	birth	dearth	hearth
7	**rein**	sane	rain	reign	pain	maim
8	**stone**	known	frown	sewn	loan	phone

Homonyms

For each of the following words write another word which **sounds exactly the same** but is spelt differently.

1	steel _____	5	boy _____	9	tale _____
2	meet _____	6	waste _____	10	missed _____
3	right _____	7	bear _____	11	foul _____
4	hose _____	8	reed _____	12	guilt _____

Use each of the words you have found in a sentence to show that you understand what each one means.

Prepositions

Write out the **prepositions** in these sentences.

1   The farmer was angry with the boys who had damaged his fence.
2   Chloe was asked to write about her favourite sport.
3   The frightened horse jumped over the five-barred gate.
4   The driver stood beside his damaged car.
5   I thanked my aunty for her present.
6   The sweets were shared among the whole class.
7   Jane ran past the finishing line in second place.
8   Tom's golf clubs are different from Paul's.
9   I sat between Gareth and Mohammed.
10 The police officer chased the thief through the narrow streets.

Joining sentences

Join the following pairs of sentences by choosing from

but	or	so
which		while

1   We stayed at the hotel. It overlooks the bay.
2   A man fell in the river. We were swimming.
3   Will you have lemonade? Do you prefer cola?
4   This story is very strange. It really happened.
5   The wind and rain stopped the cricket match. We decided to go home.

# of or off

Choose **of** or **off** to complete these sentences.

1   I saw the old man fall _____ the bus.
2   One _____ my friends caught a large pike.
3   As soon as the plane took _____ several _____ us felt ill.
4   Two _____ Mr Aitken's cows ran _____ down the road.
5   _____ course you will be goalkeeper unless the game is _____ .

Synonyms

Write down words which are in **similar** meaning to these.

1   rough _____
2   conceal _____
3   correct _____
4   prohibit _____
5   imitate _____
6   bravery _____
7   empty _____
8   circular _____
9   start _____
10 feeble _____
11 guard _____
12 aid _____

Prepositions

The **prepositions** in bold type in these sentences are not the correct ones. Rewrite the sentences using the correct prepositions.

1   The reward was shared equally **with** Paul, Simon and Andrew.

2   Shazia was eating her lunch all **to** herself.

3   The watchman came **of** duty at 7.00 am.

4   Eight comes **before** seven.

5   Terry ran **beyond** the winning posts in record time.

6   Do you live **at** a town or a village?

7   A rabbit is different in several ways **than** a hare.

8   Holly rested her elbows **onto** the desk.

9   The food was shared equally **among** the two dogs.

10   Patrick may not be **to** school this afternoon.

11   Pour the water **in** the bowl.

12   Marie hasn't received any letters **off** her friends.

Analogies

Complete these analogies which all deal with **gender**.

1   Masculine is to _____ as male is to female.

2   Prince is to princess as _____ is to queen.

3   Father is to _____ as mother is to daughter.

4   _____ is to Mrs as he is to she.

5   Boy is to girl as man is to _____ .

6   Uncle is to aunt as nephew is to _____ .

7   Actor is to actress as _____ is to waitress.

8   She is to he as her is to _____ .

9   Duke is to _____ as lord is to lady.

10   Brother is to sister as bridegroom is to _____ .

11   Sir is to madam as _____ is to witch.

12   Widow is to _____ as heroine is to hero.

there or their

Complete these sentences by writing **there** or **their**.

1 The two boys cleaned .... bicycles.
2 .... were crowds of people watching the carnival.
3 Gareth and Alison were .... with .... two friends.
4 The motorists were annoyed because .... cars had been damaged in the car park.
5 .... are too many children who have forgotten .... homework.
6 Do you think .... is any chance of Tracy and Deborah going on the coach trip with .... friends?

Adverbs from nouns

Complete the following sentences by using an **adverb** formed from the **noun** in the brackets.

1 Paolo played the piano (skill).
2 The climbers proceeded (caution) across the glacier.
3 The doctor cared (devotion) for his patients.
4 Stephanie answered the questions (sense).
5 Our school (generosity) supported the earthquake disaster appeal.

Completing sentences

Complete these sentences by choosing the correct word from the brackets.

1 Each of the boys did (their, his) best to complete the climb.
2 Every one of those houses (has, have) something wrong with (it, them).
3 Each of the hotel bedrooms (has, have) (its, their) own balcony.
4 Every one of the yachts had capsized before (it, they) finished the course.
5 Each of the labradors (has, have) been chosen to train as a guide dog.

Opposites

Write down the **opposite** of these words.

1	late	5	friend	9	out ....
2	up	6	always	10	under ....
3	different	7	from	11	short ....
4	entrance	8	success	12	deep ....

Direct speech

Write out these sentences, using **speech marks** where required.

1   Help! she screamed. The boat is sinking.

2   Please open the window, Mr Allinson said. I find it stuffy.

3   If you call me mean once more, warned Lizzie, I'll hit you.

4   Excuse me, Mrs Thomas, said Suhaib, but I think you have left your umbrella.

5   In a quiet voice Lucy asked, May I have my ball back?

6   Stay where you are! the farmer shouted to us.

7   I am very grateful for the invitation, said Michael, but I am afraid I shan't be able to accept.

8   His mother told him, You must be back by nine o'clock.

9   Have you seen my dog? the old man inquired. It ran off early this morning.

10   Yes, I did eat all the cake, admitted Andrew, but I was very hungry.

Spelling

All these words are spelt incorrectly. Write them spelt correctly.

1	peice	5	invisable	9	libary
2	allso	6	goverment	10	alltogether
3	recieve	7	excitment	11	differant
4	quantaty	8	visiter	12	developement

Opposites – prefixes

Write the **opposites** of these words by adding a **prefix**.

1	sincere	5	possible	9	welcome
2	perfect	6	order	10	honour
3	lawful	7	truthful	11	responsible
4	sense	8	allow	12	complete

Use each of the opposites you have formed in a sentence to show that you understand what each one means.

Sayings

In each of these sentences rewrite the **everyday saying** in bold type to show that you understand its meaning.

1   Are you ever **at a loose end** during the holidays?

2   If Jimmy doesn't charge he'll become **a good for nothing**.

3   It was an excellent game; the only **fly in the ointment** was that our team lost.

4   My Aunty Ellen visits us only **once in a blue moon**.

5   I think it's about time those two **buried the hatchet**.

6   **My heart was in my mouth** as I watched the trapeze artists at the circus.

7   I hope Dad doesn't **throw cold water** on our party plans.

8   I'm very pleased to know that Jenny is now **up to the mark**.

Completing sentences

Complete the following by adding interesting phrases which tell **why** something happened.

1   The helicopter could not land on the rig _____.

2   Lewis was unable to fasten his suitcase _____.

3   The plane failed to take off _____.

4   Sarah didn't return the book to the library _____.

5   None of us saw the bridge collapse _____.

6   Oliver was very upset _____.

7   There weren't any fish in the lake _____.

8   The postman couldn't get an answer _____.

9   The climbers failed to reach the summit _____.

10 Our caretaker was very annoyed _____.

Spelling

These words end in either **ible** or **able**.

1   that which can be seen

2   showing good sense

3   to be trusted or relied upon

4   awful: frightful

5   easy to carry

Picture vocabulary

Give the names of these items worn on the feet. Who would wear them? Write an interesting sentence about each.

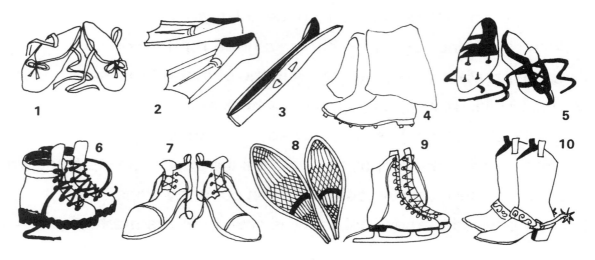

1   2   3   4   5
6   7   8   9   10

Noun groups

In the following list of nouns there are five names of **parts of the body**, five **animals** and five **buildings**. There are also five words that do not belong to any of the three groups.

Make a list of the nouns in the correct groups.

bank	rounders	badger	skull	net
school	skill	ankle	bat	wrist
factory	hotel	arm	bark	falcon
tower	wasp	scoop	neck	snail

Sayings

Explain what is meant by these **sayings**.

1   sink or swim

2   walls have ears

3   dead beat

4   out of his depth

5   sit on the fence

6   take the rough with the smooth

7   let bygones be bygones

8   a feather in your cap

9   blow your own trumpet

10   let sleeping dogs lie

Punctuation

Write out these sentences using **speech marks** and other **necessary punctuation**.

1 heres philip lets ask him to come with us said rufus

2 does mr rigby still mend clocks inquired becky

3 youre not always right you know said adrian

4 emily shouted to her mother will you answer the telephone

5 robert looked at the muddy field and said ill be surprised if we start the match

6 keep on practising maddie urged her piano teacher you will master this difficult piece

7 where does britain obtain most of its rubber asked freddie

8 is the hotel big asked james or is it a small hotel

9 the pacific said mr brady is the largest of the worlds oceans

10 stop shouted the police officer you cant go down market street because theres a burst water main

Homonyms

A Write a word which is spelt differently but **sounds the same** as the following.

1	bridal	6	seen	11	draft
2	birth	7	mussel	12	vain
3	cereal	8	kernel	13	sword
4	prophet	9	paws	14	principle
5	waist	10	would	15	cheque

B Choose any **five** of your word pairs and write sentences to show that you understand their meanings.

whose or who's

Complete these sentences by writing either **whose** or **who's**.

1   Will you tell me _____ borrowed my pen?

2   _____ coming for a game of football?

3   Will you find out _____ book this is?

4   We met Kenny _____ sister swims for Scotland.

5   Do you know _____ coming on holiday with us?

6   _____ dog is that running across the road?

7   We saw an actor _____ often in programmes on television.

8   I saw Mr Park, _____ house was damaged in a storm.

Prepositions

Complete these sentences with suitable **prepositions**.

1   My sister is very good _____ drawing.

2   Are you pleased _____ your new car?

3   I know I can rely _____ you to help.

4   I am tired _____ playing chess every night.

5   A letter arrived _____ my friend in Canada yesterday.

6   Ana apologised _____ the teacher for being late.

7   The cyclist was involved _____ an accident outside school.

8   The thirsty dog longed _____ a drink of water.

Vocabulary

Rewrite these sentences using a **better word** than <u>got</u>.

1   The firefighter **got** on the roof to rescue the kitten.

2   When we finally **got to** the station the train had gone.

3   Julie soon **got better** from her illness.

4   We **got back** from the cinema at ten o'clock.

5   The passengers **got on** the aeroplane one hour late.

6   The cook **got ready** an appetising meal.

Collective nouns

Complete the following by choosing a suitable **collective noun**.

1 a .... of bees

2 a squadron of ....

3 a .... of books

4 a .... of cows

5 an .... of soldiers

6 a .... of puppies

7 a brood of ....

8 an .... of poems

Opposites

Write the **opposites** of the following words. The last letters of the words you need are given.

1 minimum ....m

2 straight ....t

3 permanent ....y

4 pretty ....y

5 true ....e

6 no ....s

7 wise ....h

8 hollow ....d

9 victory ....t

10 senior ....r

11 opaque ....t

12 barren ....e

Take the letter of the alphabet which comes immediately before each initial letter of the words you have made. What is the message this gives?

Comprehension

On the verge of a wood within a mile of the town of Ashby was an extensive meadow. The ground sloped gradually down on all sides to a level bottom, and was enclosed for the lists with strong palisades, forming an oblong space a quarter of a mile in length and about half as broad. Strong wooden gates, each wide enough to admit two horsemen riding abreast, afforded entry for the combatants at the northern and southern ends of the lists. At each of these two heralds were stationed and a strong body of men-at-arms for maintaining order.

On a platform beyond the southern entrance were pitched five magnificent pavilions, adorned with pennons of russet and black, the chosen colours of the five knights' challengers. The northern access to the lists terminated in a similar entrance of thirty feet in breadth, outside which was a large enclosed space for such knights as intended to enter the lists with the challengers. Behind were placed tents for armourers, farriers, and other attendants ready to give their services wherever they might be necessary.

The exterior of the lists was occupied by temporary galleries for those lords and ladies who were expected to attend the tournament. A narrow space between these galleries and the lists gave accommodation for spectators of a better degree than the mere vulgar. The latter arranged themselves upon banks of turf prepared for the purpose, while many hundreds had perched themselves on the branches of trees around the meadow; even the steeple of a church at some distance was crowded with spectators.

One gallery in the very centre of the eastern side of the lists, exactly opposite to the spot where the shock of the combat was to take place, was raised higher than the others, more richly decorated, and graced by a sort of throne and canopy, on which the royal arms were emblazoned.

From *Ivanhoe* by Sir Walter Scott

1   What were the colours of the challengers?

2   Name all the viewing points for the spectators.

3   Who would keep order?

4   What are farriers?

5   What work would be done by an armourer?

6   What were the duties of the heralds?

7   Why was the royal gallery situated in that particular place?

8   What is the 'shock of the combat'?

9   How do you know that this event was very well attended?

10 Find the meanings of these words.
    palisades   pennons   gallery   canopy

11 Find words in the passage which mean the same as the following.

    a allowed   **d** not permanent
    b outside   **e** ended
    c decorated   **f** edge

12 In what century do you think the tournament could have taken place?

13 Draw a plan of the tournament field and mark all the important details.

14 Give a title to this extract.

Verbs

Use each of these **verbs** in sentences of your own.

1	limped	5	descended	9	complained
2	unfolded	6	demolished	10	believed
3	attracted	7	beckoned	11	scrambled
4	encouraged	8	challenged	12	struggled

Possession

Use the apostrophe (') to show ownership.

1	a hairdresser for men	6	a corner for pets
2	the paints of the artist	7	the voice of the singer
3	a library for children	8	the tennis rackets of the girls
4	the toys of the babies	9	the cricket bat owned by James
5	a concert for pensioners	10	the feathers of the geese

Silent letters

The answers to these clues all contain a **silent letter**. Underline the silent letter in each word.

1   Malta is an   i __ __ __ __ __
2   a fish with pink flesh
    s __ __ __ __ __
3   to hear carefully
    l __ __ __ __ __ __
4   a garden ornament
    g __ __ __ __
5   not right   w __ __ __ __
6   a war plane   b __ __ __ __ __

7   a joint in the fingers
    k __ __ __ __ __ __
8   a tree growing in hot countries
    p __ __ __
9   a large cat with spots
    l __ __ __ __ __ __
10 where things are stored
    d __ __ __ __ __

Nouns from verbs

Form **nouns** from these verbs.

1	arrive	6	donate	11	capture
2	punish	7	memorise	12	applaud
3	move	8	destroy	13	believe
4	complain	9	imagine	14	alter
5	depart	10	enlarge	15	conclude

Answers

Page 2 Picture vocabulary
1 kangaroo 2 walrus 3 bat 4 beaver
5 whale 6 tiger 7 platypus 8 skunk
9 elephant 10 rhino 11 giraffe 12 polar
bear 13 gorilla 14 koala 15 zebra
16 squirrel 17 camel 18 mouse 19 hippo
20 porcupine

Page 3 Pronouns
A 1 he 2 We, they 3 He, me, he 4 I, her,
she, me 5 them, me 6 She, they, her
7 you, him 8 They, him, they, us 9 She, it,
her 10 He, he, it
B 1 hers 2 mine 3 ours 4 his 5 theirs
6 yours
C 1 they 2 him 3 it 4 us 5 you, her

Page 4 Alphabetical order
A 1 tank, tent, thermometer, tiger, tractor
2 pan, pity, plum, polish, pull, pygmy
3 hawk, help, high, hobby, huge, hymn
4 fair, fear, field, flat, foot, funny
5 wash, week, whirl, witch, worm, wrote
B 1 cage, calendar, camel, castle, caterpillar
2 baboon, banana, barley, basket, bath, bay
3 factory, fail, fall, family, fan, fast
4 habit, hair, ham, harp, hatch, hawk
5 meat, meet, mellow, mend, merge,
message
C 1 forbid, forfeit, forget, fork, form, forward
2 patch, paternal, path, patience, patrol,
patter
3 cancel, candid, cane, canoe, canvas,
canyon
4 manager, mane, mankind, manly, manor,
mansion

Page 5 Picture vocabulary
1 bicycle 2 hot air balloon 3 van 4 sledge
5 hovercraft 6 plane 7 car 8 boat 9 bus
10 helicopter 11 canoe 12 train 13 tanker
14 shuttle 15 motorbike
Check your child's five descriptions.

Page 6 Vocabulary – associations
A 1 fish 2 army 3 history 4 storage
5 aircraft 6 birds 7 fruit 8 artist 9 water
10 oil 11 ship 12 grapes
B 1 headteacher 2 captain 3 principal
4 keeper 5 director 6 governor

7 president 8 editor 9 judge 10 conductor
C 1 dictionary 2 autobiography 3 atlas
4 diary/journal 5 anthology 6 log book
7 scrap book 8 encyclopaedia 9 telephone
directory 10 album

Page 7 Verbs – sounds
A 1–6 Check that your child has chosen an
appropriate verb for each sentence.
B 1–8 Check that your child's sound words
are suitable.
C 1–8 Check that your child's words are
suitable.
D 1–4 Check your child's sentences.

Page 8 Spelling
1 weight 2 niece 3 neighbour 4 shriek
5 mischief 6 deceive 7 retrieve 8 ceiling
9 foreign 10 reindeer 11 ancient 12 receipt
13 seize 14 cashier 15 conceit 16 chief

Vocabulary
1–6 Check that your child's words are
suitable for their sentence.

Punctuation
1 Clive, Paul and Craig play golf every
Saturday and Sunday.
2 Mrs Marsden told Jasmine to take the
cakes to Aunty Margaret.
3 In our Easter holidays we went to London
and saw Buckingham Palace and the Bank
of England.
4 His friends, who were becoming anxious,
telephoned Leeds police station.
A police officer soon arrived.
5 For Sunday lunch Billy and Rob had
pork chops, cabbage, carrots and roast
potatoes.

Page 9 Abbreviations
1 The National Society for the Prevention of
Cruelty to Children
2 United States of America
3 Royal National Lifeboat Institute
4 Company
5 Royal National Institute for the Blind
6 World Wildlife Fund/World Wide Fund for
Nature
7 International Monetary Fund

8 North Atlantic Treaty Organisation
9 United Kingdom
10 Genetically Modified
11 Limited
12 Kilometres

Opposites
1 arrive
2 often
3 poverty
4 innocent
5 gradual
6 maximum
7 fertile
8 advance
9 minority
10 still
11 illegal
12 external

Synonyms
Examples: 1 begin/start **2** dear **3** outside
4 cure **5** huge **6** level **7** savage/cruel
8 cheeky **9** allow **10** forsake **11** copy
12 clear/translucent

Homonyms
1 saw or soar **2** meddle **3** quay **4** wrap
5 route **6** weight **7** bridal **8** peddle **9** aisle
10 principal **11** dough **12** sealing

Page 10 Adjectives
A 1–10 Check that your child's adjectives are suitable to complete the sentence.
B 1 gigantic **2** brilliant **3** beautiful
4 miserable **5** icy **6** towering
C 1–10 Check your child's adjectives are opposite in meaning to those given.

Page 11 Spelling and vocabulary
A 1 seaweed **2** shoal **3** submarine **4** shark
5 scuba diver
B 1 exercise **2** explored **3** extended
4 extracted **5** expensive
C 1 fruit **2** vegetable **3** shape **4** metal
5 ocean
D 1–5 Check that your child's words are suitable.

Page 12 Vocabulary
A 1 stetson – a cowboy **2** hard hat – miner
3 wig – judge **4** fire helmet – firefighter **5** space helmet – astronaut **6** nurse's hat – nurse
B 1 grains **2** abbreviations **3** freshwater fish **4** surnames **5** rodents **6** insects

7 herbs **8** woods
C 1 office **2** galley **3** safe or vault
4 cabin **5** cell

Page 13 Indirect speech
1 Danny said that his football boots needed new laces.
2 The policewoman said to my dad that he wasn't allowed to park his car in this street.
3 Heather asked if the train to Walsall had gone.
4 Aunty Shirley said to me that she hoped I liked my birthday present.
5 I asked the librarian if she had a copy of *Oliver Twist*.
6 Marian said that she goes swimming twice a week.
7 Mr Toms snapped at Bobby that he was afraid he wasn't working hard enough to pass the exam.
8 The teacher asked Freya if she would please bring the tape recorder.
9 George said that I was a slow coach and we would miss the bus if we didn't hurry.
10 Milly said to George that she was sorry but she was running as fast as she could.

Present and past tense
1 gave **2** knew **3** caught **4** felt **5** left
6 swam **7** struck **8** laid **9** began **10** drank
11 throw **12** forget **13** build **14** ring
15 steal **16** bring **17** hold **18** shake
19 drive **20** fly

Page 14 Direct speech
1 Simon asked, "How tall are you?"
2 My mum asked, "Are you ready for tea?"
3 Elizabeth shouted to Saira, "Be quick!"
4 The mechanic told Mr Barnes, "Your car will be ready on Tuesday."
5 Tilly's mother asked her, "Have you finished your homework?"
6 Paul told his dad, "I've been chosen to play for the school cricket team."
7 Dean asked Mark, "Do you want to go fishing?"
8 Mrs Bladen told her son, Andrew, "You must not miss the last bus home."
9 Harry Cox shouted, "I'm trapped on my roof!"
10 Mr Green asked David, "Clean the windows and brush the floor."

Incorrect sentences

1 The dog and the cat **were** lying on the carpet.
2 Malcolm **taught** me to play badminton.
3 Was it her or him **who** spoke to you?
4 Dawn could not see her dog **anywhere**.
5 You can **borrow** my bicycle if you're careful.
6 Patrick **caught two** perch in the canal.
7 The reward was **shared among** the three **boys**.
8 Have you **spoken** to your father?
9 My brother was taller.
10 Neither the boys nor the girls **have** finished **their** work.

Page 15 Picture story
Check that your child's story explains what is happening in the pictures.

Page 16 Contractions
1 must not 2 that is 3 I will 4 we have
5 you are 6 who would 7 where is
8 would not 9 she will 10 they have
11 will not 12 they will
13 there would 14 it is 15 we will

Vocabulary
1 did 2 saw 3 who 4 I 5 those 6 teach
7 where, were 8 seen, saw 9 me
10 too, to, two

Adjectives
1 warmer 2 less 3 most, honest
4 cleverer 5 cosiest 6 more generous

Page 17 Plurals
1 Yesterday the workmen repaired the roofs.
2 I saw calves, horses, geese, and donkeys on the farm.
3 The policewomen caught the thieves in the act.
4 The old ladies twisted their ankles on the stony beaches.
5 The boys fell off the rocks and hurt themselves.
6 My cousins came to see us last weekend.
7 The girls' pencils were in the boxes.
8 The school plays weren't very well acted.
9 The postmen delivered letters and parcels to houses in the valleys.
10 We do not think you understand the problems.

Spelling
1 We all laughed at the puppy's **behaviour**.

2 Jenny was very **tearful** when she fell off her bicycle.
3 I saw the rabbit **disappear** down that hole.
4 Neither John nor Betty has **completed** the work.
5 The policeman **seized** the frightened dog.
6 **Although** he was near exhaustion, Oliver finished the race.
7 Heather replied **sensibly** to the teacher's questions.
8 There was a **beautiful** display of roses in the entrance hall.
9 In warm weather Amelia **always** wears sandals.
10 Mum knitted a **woollen** jersey.

Page 18 Vocabulary – verb association
A 1 to conceal – hide 2 to demolish – pull or tear down; destroy 3 to substitute – replace one thing or person with another
4 to suppress – put an end to; stop by force
5 to excavate – scoop out; uncover by digging 6 to investigate – search into; examine closely 7 to erupt – burst
8 to refine – make pure
B 1 suppressed 2 erupted 3 excavated
4 refined 5 substituted
C 1–5 Check your child's answers.

Page 19 Spelling and vocabulary
A 1 pianist 2 scientist 3 novelist
4 parachutist 5 ventriloquist 6 soloist
7 optimist
B 1 attic 2 attempt 3 attack 4 attractive
5 attach
C 1 puncture 2 temperature 3 capture
4 furniture 5 torture
D 1 quarrel 2 mirror 3 surrender 4 terrier
5 quarry

Page 20 Analogies
1 stable 2 fur 3 trumpet 4 ewe 5 hare
6 sett 7 hiss 8 fish

Verbs
Examples: 1 attack 2 suffering 3 enters
4 chase 5 persevere 6 fall

Vocabulary
1 applause 2 summit 3 spectator 4 famine
5 glacier

Page 21 Pronouns
A 1 yourself 2 myself 3 yourselves
4 herself 5 himself

B 1 You – Steven 2 it – hurricane 3 they – Paul and Sally 4 her – Jacqueline 5 me – Mr Morris

C 1 we 2 ourselves 3 they 4 theirs 5 us 6 mine 7 me 8 her/his 9 yourself 10 itself

Page 22 Contractions

1 Where've 2 doesn't 3 You'd 4 won't 5 can't 6 don't 7 I'd, you'd 8 shan't 9 I'll, they're 10 They've, it's

Incorrect sentences

1 My brother **taught** me how to ride a bike.
2 Ava acted **well** in the play.
3 Seamus wouldn't give me **any** of his toffees.
4 There **are** a lot of mountains in Austria.
5 Terry ran home as **quickly** as he could.
6 A man and his dog **were** waiting outside the shop.
7 Betsy could not come **any** quicker.
8 Your fishing rod is different **from** mine.
9 He **wants** to go tomorrow.
10 The group **sang** the same song twice.
11 Poor Lesley couldn't remember **anything**.
12 Between you and **me**, I don't think he is the right choice for captain.

Page 23 Vocabulary

1 feeling 2 exercising 3 gem 4 dwelling 5 time

Jumbled letters

1 owl 2 heron 3 kiwi 4 parrot 5 thrush 6 eagle

Associations

set A 1 photographer – camera 2 jockey – saddle 3 referee – whistle 4 doctor – stethoscope 5 conductor – baton 6 mechanic – spanner 7 decorator – brush
set B 1 actress – theatre 2 keeper – zoo 3 chemist – laboratory 4 astronomer – observatory 5 administrator – office 6 chef – kitchen 7 artist – studio

Page 24 Adverbs

A 1 regularly 2 dejectedly, loudly 3 now, soon 4 excitedly 5 angrily 6 everywhere, sadly 7 anywhere, sadly 8 always, well 9 away, loudly 10 once, frantically 11 never 12 twice

B These answers are just a guide. Check that your child has used a suitable adverb in each sentence.

1 thoroughly 2 badly 3 immediately 4 vividly 5 regularly 6 around 7 excitedly 8 softly 9 nastily 10 badly 11 attentively 12 suddenly 13 easily 14 around 15 greedily 16 patiently

Page 25 Opposites

1 Alan's invention was a **success**.
2 The yacht sailed through the **calm** seas.
3 Sarah checked the time as she **entered** the office.
4 It was **impossible** for the mountain to be climbed.
5 Bobby **denied** that he had left the tap running.
6 The passengers were very **annoyed** when the plane was delayed.
7 Our teacher was **encouraged** by our exam results.
8 About one third of Jayne's answers were **incorrect**.
9 The **minority** of our class come to school by bus.
10 Tom helped his Dad to push the car **backwards**.

Vocabulary

1 We managed to **extinguish** the fire.
2 Workmen have **erected** a bus shelter in our street.
3 You can do it! Don't be **discouraged** by their failure.
4 You will have to **save** some money for your holidays.
5 The old lady couldn't **tolerate** the loud noise of the machines any longer.
6 After losing a sail in a violent storm, the yacht **entered** port for repairs.
7 Sally was **annoyed** by the way her friends behaved towards her.
8 The football match was **postponed** because of the frozen ground.

Page 26 Verbs

1 lubricate 2 narrate 3 meditate 4 cultivate 5 dilate 6 imitate 7 rotate 8 educate 9 relate 10 emigrate

Completing sentences

1 neither, nor 2 whether, or 3 If, then 4 such, that 5 Either, or 6 so, that

Spelling

definite, February, necessary, separate, believe, Wednesday, present, seize, skilful, eight/eighth

Page 27 Singular

1 The window has been cleaned.
2 This boy wishes to play chess.
3 I was hoping to finish the painting last Monday.
4 The lady checked her watch.
5 The policewoman arrested the thief.
6 I don't think you can catch the mouse.
7 The chimpanzee is an intelligent animal.
8 My cousin is coming on holiday with my family.

Completing sentences

1–8 Check that your child's answers explain where the action is taking place.

Spelling

1 sour **2** court **3** harbour **4** journalist **5** encourage **6** neighbour **7** journey **8** armour

Page 28 Joining phrases

1 so **2** but **3** or **4** but **5** so **6** and **7** but **8** because **9** unless **10** while

Incorrect sentences

1 She ran home as **quickly** as she could.
2 My radio battery is **worn** out.
3 There is a cat and a dog **in** our front garden.
4 The boy has **broken** his leg.
5 My fingers ache and I cannot write **any** more.
6 "Please pass me **those** books," said Graham.
7 "I **saw** the boy run over the field," said the caretaker.
8 The teacher thought Michael **did** it.
9 **Weren't** they pleased when they knew we were coming?
10 Every one of us **has** an equal chance **of** reaching the final.

Rhyming words

made, weighed, played, raid;   toes, grows, chose, froze;   some, become, crumb, glum; smear, near, cheer, sphere;   home, foam, comb, dome

Page 29 Questions

1–10 Check your child's answers.

Homonyms

1 dyed **2** ewes **3** told **4** fined **5** sown **6** heel **7** sewn **8** practice **9** practise

Similes

1 a mule **2** a kitten **3** an ox **4** a dove **5** a peacock **6** a bat **7** a deer **8** an owl

Page 30 Pronouns

1 your **2** his **3** mine **4** theirs **5** yours **6** its **7** their **8** my **9** mine **10** our, its

your or you're

1 you're **2** your **3** your, you're **4** you're, your **5** you're, you're, your

Vocabulary

1 cat **2** replace **3** commence **4** cousin **5** stroll **6** climb **7** hotel **8** grass **9** heat **10** holly

Page 31 Verbs

A 1 offered, lend **2** ran, finished **3** called, went **4** comes, whistle **5** Run, play, suggested **6** ate, dug, cut, trimmed **7** come, read, said **8** tossed, struck, sank **9** rode, fell, cut **10** swerved, scored
B 1 weep **2** cure **3** walk **4** touch **5** rise **6** quack **7** kick **8** wade **9** twirl **10** listen **11** rotate **12** obey **13** mend **14** grasp **15** finish **16** amble **17** subtract **18** purchase **19** nibble **20** surrender

Page 32 Adjectives

A 1 downcast, muddy, first
2 two, considerate, elderly, busy
3 continuous, sandy, dismal
4 four, experienced, sheer, slippery
5 impressive, three, triumphant, American, successful, vast
6 heavy, grey, torrential, exciting
B 1 agonizing **2** wicked **3** incomparable **4** colossal **5** gorgeous
C 1–15 Check you child's answers.

Page 33 Spelling

disappear, chocolate, secondary, address, calendar, temperature, detach, cupboard, miniature, parliament, miscellaneous, marvellous

Comparing adjectives

1 tall, **taller, tallest 2** safe, **safer, safest 3** heavy, **heavier, heaviest 4** noisy, **noisier, noisiest 5** honest, **more honest, most honest 6** intelligent, **more intelligent, most intelligent 7** good, **better, best 8** old, **older, oldest 9** bad, **worse, worst 10** thoughtful, **more thoughtful, most thoughtful**

Vocabulary

A **1** enter **2** ascend **3** retreat **4** descend
5 crawl **6** advance **7** leave **8** follow
B **1–6** Check your child's answers.

Pages 34–35 Comprehension

1a Salonica **b** south
2 Yes (Check your child's answer for the reasons to support this.)
3 He is terrified; the last voice he heard was of a guard.
4 He wasn't used to voices.
5 They sat down to smoke a cigarette.
6 Their speech was very different to the man that David was used to.
7 David thought he had seen the van before at the camp
8 The sound of the van caused David to 'stiffen'.
9 "David's feet were no longer part of him" "...his feet followed their own path independently..." and "his feet carried him over the bridge."
10 Check your child's answer and the reasons to support this.
11 Check your child's title is suitable for the extract.
12 Check that your child has understood the meaning of the phrases.
13 Check your child's sentences.
14 Check you child's answers, e.g. **a** adverbs – independently, noiselessly, confidently **b** prepositions – over, up, of **c** common nouns – feet, bridge, teeth **d** pronouns – him, he, it **e** verbs – cared, avoided, whispered **f** adjectives – over and over, different, difficult

Page 36 Verbs

1–8 Check your child's verbs are suitable.

Rhyming words

1 height **2** same **3** bough **4** streak **5** pier
6 hearth **7** maim **8** frown

Homonyms

1 steal **2** meat **3** write **4** hoes **5** buoy
6 waist **7** bare **8** read **9** tail **10** mist
11 fowl **12** gilt

Page 37 Prepositions

1 with **2** to, about **3** over **4** beside **5** for
6 among **7** in **8** from **9** between
10 through

Joining sentences

1 We stayed at the hotel which overlooks the bay.
2 A man fell into the river while we were swimming.
3 Will you have lemonade or do you prefer cola?
4 This story is very strange but it really happened.
5 The wind and rain stopped the cricket match so we decided to go home.

Of or off

1 I saw the old man fall off the bus.
2 One of my friends caught a large pike.
3 As soon as the plane took off several of us felt ill.
4 Two of Mr Aitken's cows ran off down the road.
5 Of course you will be goalkeeper unless the game is off.

Synonyms

1 uneven **2** hide **3** right **4** forbid **5** copy
6 courage **7** void **8** round **9** begin
10 weak **11** defend **12** help

Page 38 Prepositions

1 The reward was shared equally **among** Paul, Simon and Andrew.
2 Shazia was eating her lunch all **by** herself.
3 The watchman came **off** duty at 7. 00 am.
4 Eight comes **after** seven.
5 Terry ran **through** the winning posts in record time.
6 Do you live **in** a town or a village?
7 A rabbit is different in several ways **from** a hare.
8 Holly rested her elbows **on** the desk.
9 The food was shared equally **between** the two dogs.
10 Patrick may not be **at** school this afternoon.
11 Pour the water **into** the bowl.
12 Marie hasn't received any letters **from** her friends.

Analogies

1 feminine **2** king **3** son **4** Mr **5** woman
6 niece **7** waiter **8** him **9** duchess **10** bride
11 wizard **12** widower

Page 39 there or their

1 their **2** There **3** there, their **4** their
5 There, their **6** there, their

Adverbs from nouns
1 Paolo played the piano **skilfully**.
2 The climbers proceeded **cautiously** across the glacier.
3 The doctor cared **devoutly** for his patients.
4 Stephanie answered the questions **sensibly**.
5 Our school **generously** supported the earthquake disaster appeal.

Completing sentences
1 his 2 has, it 3 has, its 4 it 5 has

Opposites
1 early 2 down 3 same 4 exit 5 enemy
6 never 7 to 8 failure 9 in 10 over 11 long
12 shallow

Page 40 Direct speech
1 "Help!" she screamed. "The boat is sinking."
2 "Please open the window," Mr Allinson said. "I find it stuffy."
3 "If you call me mean once more," warned Lizzie, "I'll hit you."
4 "Excuse me, Mrs Thomas," said Suhaib, "but I think you have left your umbrella."
5 In a quiet voice Lucy asked, "May I have my ball back?"
6 "Stay where you are!" The farmer shouted to us.
7 "I am very grateful for the invitation," said Michael, "but I am afraid I shan't be able to accept."
8 His mother told him, "You must be back by nine o'clock."
9 "Have you seen my dog?" the old man inquired. "It ran off early this morning."
10 "Yes, I did eat all the cake," admitted Andrew, "but I was very hungry."

Spelling
1 piece 2 also 3 receive 4 quantity
5 invisible 6 government 7 excitement
8 visitor 9 library 10 altogether
11 different 12 development

Opposites – prefixes
1 insincere 2 imperfect 3 unlawful
4 nonsense 5 impossible 6 disorder
7 untruthful 8 disallow 9 unwelcome
10 dishonour 11 irresponsible
12 incomplete
Check your child's sentences.

Page 41 Sayings
1 bored/have nothing to do 2 irresponsible or worthless person 3 a flaw that detracts from enjoyment 4 very rarely 5 make up 6 very anxious 7 ruin 8 able to achieve something

Completing sentences
1–10 Check that your child's answers are suitable.

Spelling
1 visible 2 sensible 3 responsible/reliable
4 terrible 5 portable

Page 42 Picture vocabulary
1 ballet shoes – a ballet dancer
2 flippers – a sea diver
3 skis – a skier
4 waders – a fisherman
5 spikes – a track runner
6 hiking boots – a walker/hiker
7 clown boots – a clown
8 snow shoes – an Inuit
9 ice skates – an ice-skater
10 cowboy boots – a cowboy

Noun groups
Parts of the body ankle, arm, skull, neck, wrist
Animals wasp, badger, bat, falcon, snail
Buildings bank, factory, tower, hotel, school rounders, scoop, bark, net

Sayings
1 to either succeed or fail 2 secrets will escape 3 tired/exhausted 4 can't cope with a situation 5 not to take sides in an argument 6 with every good thing that happens there is always a bad thing and this needs to be accepted 7 don't hold grudges 8 an achievement 9 to brag and self congratulate 10 don't bring up old grudges or past disagreements

Page 43 Punctuation
1 "Here's Philip. Let's ask him to come with us." said Rufus.
2 "Does Mr Rigby still mend clocks?" inquired Becky.
3 "You're not always right, you know," said Adrian.
4 Emily shouted to her mother, "Will you answer the telephone!"
5 Robert looked at the muddy field and said, "I'll be surprised if we start the match."

6 "Keep on practising Maddie," urged her piano teacher, "you will master this difficult piece."
7 "Where does Britain obtain most of its rubber?" asked Freddie.
8 "Is the hotel big," asked James, "or is it a small hotel?"
9 "The Pacific," said Mr Brady, "is the largest of the world's oceans."
10 "Stop!" shouted the police officer, "you can't go down Market Street because there's a burst water main."

Homonyms
A 1 bridle 2 berth 3 serial 4 profit 5 waste
6 scene 7 muscle 8 colonel 9 pause
10 wood 11 draught 12 vein 13 soared
14 principal 15 check
B Check your child's answers.

Page 44 Whose or who's
1 who's 2 Who's 3 whose 4 whose
5 who's 6 Whose 7 who's 8 whose

Prepositions
1 at 2 with 3 on 4 with/of 5 from 6 to 7 in
8 for

Vocabulary
1–6 Check your child's answers.

Page 45 Collective nouns
1 swarm 2 aircraft 3 library 4 herd
5 army 6 litter 7 chickens 8 anthology

Opposites
1 maximum 2 bent 3 temporary 4 ugly
5 false 6 yes 7 foolish 8 solid 9 defeat
10 junior 11 transparent 12 fertile
Secret message: last exercise

Pages 46–47 Comprehension
1 russet and black
2 lists, galleries, banks of turf, branches of trees, the steeple of a church and the royal gallery
3 Men-at-arms would keep order at the entrances.
4 A farrier is a person who shoes horses.
5 An armourer makes and mends armour.
6 The duties of the heralds was to open the wooden gates.
7 They were situated there because it offered a less shocking view of the combat.
8 The blood and gore of the fight.
9 Because people had to climb trees and watch from the church steeple therefore it must be overcrowded.
10 palisades – a strong fence made of stakes driven into the ground
pennons – a long flag
gallery – an upper level of seating
canopy – a roofed structure serving as shelter
11a afforded b beyond c adorned
d temporary e terminated f verge
12 Check your child's answer.
13 Check your child's drawing.
14 Check that your child's title is suitable for the extract.

Page 48 Verbs
1–12 Check your child's use of verbs.

Possession
1 a men's hairdressers 2 the artist's paints
3 a children's library 4 the babies' toys
5 a pensioners' concert 6 a pets' corner
7 the singer's voice 8 the girls' tennis rackets 9 James's cricket bat 10 the geese's feathers

Silent letters
1 island 2 salmon 3 listen 4 gnome
5 wrong 6 bomber 7 knuckle 8 palm
9 leopard 10 drawer

Nouns from verbs
1 arrival 2 punishment 3 movement
4 complaint 5 departure 6 donation
7 memory 8 destruction 9 imagination
10 enlargement 11 captive 12 applause
13 belief 14 alteration 15 conclusion

Published by Collins
An imprint of HarperCollinsPublishers Ltd
1 London Bridge Street
London
SE1 9GF

First published in 1978
This edition first published in 2012

© Derek Newton and David Smith 2012

10 9 8 7 6

ISBN 978-0-00-750546-3

The authors assert their moral right to be identified as the authors of this work.

British Library Cataloguing in Publication data.

A CIP record of this book is available from the British Library.

Every effort has been made to trace copyright holders and to obtain their permission for the use of copyright material. The authors and publishers will gladly receive any information enabling them to rectify any error or omission in subsequent editions.

Project managed by Katie Galloway
Production by Rebecca Evans
Page layout by Exemplarr Worldwide Ltd
Illustrated by A. Rodger
Printed by Martins the Printers